SOONER

SOONER

MARGARET CHRISTAKOS

Coach House Books

Published with the assistance of the Canada Council for the Arts and the Ontario Arts
Council. We also acknowledge the financial support of the Government of Canada
through the Book Publishing Industry Development Program (BPDIP).

LIBRARY AND ARCHIVES CANADA CATALOGUING IN PUBLICATION

Christakos, Margaret
    Sooner / Margaret Christakos.

Poems.
ISBN 1-55245-159-3

    I. Title.

PS8555.H675S66 2005   C811'.54   C2005-905082-9

And if this is the ending
you know how you got here

CONTENTS

GRASS

Sugar driver

If there was a place in her body that could
turn to ice then melt again she might have seen

the point of walking forehead-first into the restaurant whose air
conditioning charged one with the sense of a balloon-shaped planet

whistling oxygen at alarming speed The park attracted her lungs
with a movement of green shadow She laid her body

                        on the grass like a wrestler felled by brute force
                        A bird passed over her nostrils and she flinched not

                        liking the proximity of the arse of the creature to
                        her insides even if there was no imminent danger or

                        pollution even if she knew she was ridiculous Many moments
                        in her life were like this Evening was digested like

a thirty-seventh birthday as if something momentous both had and
failed to happen producing benign indulgence of the sameness of

things and turgid resentment that life should not shock her
with its pleasures After all someone was getting the good

bits of it this very moment every minute and why
should it not be her Her own fortune spread its

digits in the weeds and soil from which a quantity
of dog excrement had recently been lifted The dirt of

yesterday evanesced and everyone was comfortable with this feature of
nature Overhead a helicopter rattled to the children's hospital squelching

the small victim's moans She winced at how the sun
knifed the air jagging off the silver blades As if

the machine could cross over into a parallel realm to
a mountain of abducted innocence The innocence of a mountainous

abduction where things simply moved from life to death and
one had only to be grateful for compressed file folders

of enumerable experiences which could be described as belonging to
or being of the person's own making and keeping Her

                  waist flinched at the moist strand of mucus issuing from
                      a snail's clumsy suction cup but to kill the thing

                  would be unjust and even embarrassing Was she so unsettled
                  by the real So unhinged by the expectable hingedness of

                  animal bodies to human life Sometimes you could not prevent
                  disgust Ants and worms crickets beetles slugs traipsed past sand

cement brick paths gravel bench legs to get to fresh
dander of her skin enmeshed with dog-shit palimpsest The heat

was considerable for eight PM As if the ground memorized
everything that happened above it and spent the night feeling

bad then a little better then okay again by dawn
for the whole bruising transfusion to reoccur If the child

                              died the parents would have to live with it She
                              watched the sky pitch to dusk A pall of electric

                         leakage hissed into the pink bowl of the parkette The
                         beige triangle of a man's chin approached One booted leg

                              went over her ribs She stared into his crotch He
                              sat on her laughing how it was time didn't she

realize she would be late for the newscast Was she
not feeling well Wasn't the grass cold Her kidneys could

fail from the dampness besides a couple of children were
staring imagining she was dead With both palms she pushed

the man's knees backward Her thighs crumpled toward her chest
and she rocked on the lumps of her spine until

                          the momentum lifted her half upright He grabbed for her
      ·   shoulders She turned on her hands and pushed off from

                        the grass and ran toward the intersection The square sign
                  in the restaurant door flipped to CLOSED The child's heart

        monitor flatlined A green-masked crew of medical professionals sped their
                  actions liking a good challenge The parents clung to the

clipboard on which their child's allergies and contact numbers were
neatly pencilled onto specific oblong blanks She hollered for the

group of thin teenaged girls in a dusty blue hatchback
to open up the back door quickly but they fidgeted

with dark sunglasses and stepped on the gas The man
shook his arms at the slate grey patch of sky

                    above him yelling I can't believe you would miss the
                    news you of all people She ran for the newspaper

                    box and blocked his view of her She spun on
                    her heels and jogged south to the next corner The

                    child arrested and a tube was introduced The helicopter pilot
                    had a third smoke and spoke on his cellphone to

his girlfriend about the great sexual encounter they could have
with a prostitute if she trusted him enough The man

looked around himself in the parkette and realized the children
had left She sensed her blood congeal on its way

from heart to lungs as if she were a mixture
of yogourt and orange juice placed in a tray of

            cylindrical compartments The freezer worked twice as hard as the
                  fridge to achieve a result four times more removed from

            the natural softness of the summer evening Her steps slowed
                  and she felt she would fall asleep standing in the

            plain undomesticated air of the street She began to meld
                  toward lawns as if lawns were the most solid parent

No news is good news said the husband to the
weeping mother bereft in surgery chairs One has to be

willing to wait even to pray for the news when
it comes to be good or better than one had

hoped for The girls sped around the corner and felt
their slim breasts compress against each other's upper arms and

mouths graze the pasture of each other's fragrant earlobes Do
you fear for that woman's safety the one in the

orange Kangol cap asked suddenly struck Don't worry the streets
are full of freaks said the driver her long fingernails

tapping against the steering wheel languidly crossing over as if
showing off her manicure The man shoved his hands against

his groin She scurried into the shade of a large
maple The husband placed his hands around his wife's beet-red

ears The pilot took a piss shaking his chin Why
couldn't love be simpler The child's blood turned the colour

of poplar Two doctors ordered hamburgers no mayo no onion
side of coleslaw Eat your own bracchias said the nurse

I'm having fries and a jumbo Coke She squeezed her
knees into trunk bark hoisting herself onto the largest branch

ducked down breathing hard He ambled around a corner whistling
and picking his teeth The sky flickered with lost planes

and the wail of an ambulance Nobody knew how long
a night was once it started The popsicles hardened like

candy and the children unslipped two And then bed called
their mom from downstairs No fooling around Yes Mom they

said plugging their mouths with the cold treats The girlfriend
lowered her brow into the bathroom mirror and touched her

own nipples The woman's calf cramped He spotted an odd
motion This is better than maple syrup said the dead

child floating toward a cloud Why us moaned his parents
Is that you The man's pace quickened as if chasing

a lame cat She imagined herself becoming small like a
single leaf She saw the impossibility of hiding her own

uniqueness A whole life's work toward the perfect partner crashed
to the runway Both had frozen lips and tried kissing

the window Ouch Get away What the fuck do you
want from me she complained I don't want your news

nor to hear more shrill beseeching I want the frayed
swishing tapestry of flora you promised Do you hear me

Are you blind radioed the pilot Are you sleeping said
the mother Are you nuts said the man I wouldn't

        hurt you for all the grass in England Begin descent
        said the radio It is safe to land Everybody's in.

LUCENT

Better is always walking

For the sky was red and the subway shuttled from
its tunnel and out one oblong window he saw it,

a solitary shimmering carmine-edged cloud afloat in an oozing rouge
pond. Around him, people hunched into their bellies, pulling from

the public gaze all the intensity they had invited over
the afternoon in their offices. He looked at his hands,

cracked and small-knuckled. He pretended to read the corporate posters
while snatching glimpses of the upturns and sunken wounds of

people's tired eyelines, the glowing skin of one girl, the
tragicomic beard of a fleshy-cheeked college kid up too late

the night before. Who was his father and how must
he love this large boy of his now? In his

own skin he felt both beautiful and completely unprepared. He
hadn't brushed his hair, he hadn't washed. His last shower

was Tuesday – no, Sunday. Five days. But he didn't emit
an odour, and felt protected by the pall of ordinariness

which kept others from looking at him too closely, scrutinizing
his features. He'd always been interfered with in public space

and enjoyed slipping by incognito whenever possible. Without children on
the subway, people couldn't ogle him easily. He became an

anonymous middle-aged male again, no longer a teenager or young
man whose body was open property. He had a seal

around him like a second skin, and an impertinent gaze
of his own to cast upon particular female passengers, the

ones who would have intimidated him in his youth. He
tried to summon works of literature to his mind, political

ideas, mathematical quizzes, but could not distract himself from the
radiant motion of sex wafting through his mind and body,

the lucidity of his appetite. How stupid he had become,
reduced to its pressured urges. Here he was among other

adults his general age, adherents to the accepted culture of
detachment, all clothed in hundreds of dollars of well-chosen coordinates,

flickering their eyes assiduously away from each other's essential physical
self. A bunch of naked fuckers, all laced and bound

away from desire, as focused as eagles on the next
task to achieve, groceries to buy, appointments to keep, disdain

to project. It was as if every one of them
had dedicated him- or herself to the annihilation of the

public at large, that there should simply be no community
of unfamiliar humans, that if one didn't know the person

sitting in the next seat that one should assume the
living unit there to be as sentient as a car.

One looked at the shine of the bumper, the onomatopoiea
of the licence plate – all the labels read one by

one, an identity-assemblage – the value-peaking accessories. But wiped out the
real flesh and blood, wiped them out until their sheen

of absence reflected the sudden sleek red sky like metal.
In a streaming ray of light, dust filtered up off

the strangers' coats and hairdos. Several lawyer-types talked into the
void of their cellphone handsets, which were merely small pads

pressed to their own ears, without any mouthpieces at all.
It was the perfect era for an insane talkaholic; even

he could have charaded, holding two fingers up to the
side of his head, and started speaking about bathroom renovations,

or, more likely, what time it was and how soon
he would arrive at a certain destination, and what obstacles

he anticipated en route and how the weather had progressed,
and now how the train was in a tunnel again

causing the sound to fail and perhaps that he'd talk
to his respondent in a couple of minutes because the

train was suctioning air quickly, back to normal compression, and
he anticipated that he would arrive as he had projected

a couple of minutes earlier, and that his respondent should
take it easy, that he loved her, and would see

said person in a few short moments above-ground. Several conversations
of the sort ended as though a conducter had swooped

them to a skilled decrescendo, and the train pulled into
the cavernous yellow space at the city's retail flashpoint. Suddenly

everyone rose to their feet and looked directly upon the
body and face of one person whom they had been

tacitly ignoring during the ride, with a look that was
like high-gear seduction, then swung themselves by one snootily extended

forefinger and thumb around the greaseprinted silver pole and exited.
He watched them go, especially the radiant girl whose hair

at the back was tapered and wisped to look as
though she'd just gotten out of bed as naturalistically endowed

and fresh to the world as a four-year-old, and the
boy whose buttocks were visually halved by a thick black

belt charged with holding in place a massive pair of
orange parachute pants. His hands were fidgeting with both earlobes,

realizing he'd left the house without his moonstones, and disappointment
snowed through him for a moment. What an impression he

might have made just then, with the earrings. One hand
flitted to his breastbone, ah yes, there at least was

the blue medallion hanging from the slender silver chain. And
his shoes were contemporary enough, black chunks of assertive yet

youthful shitkickingness, with a counterpointing touch of the gamine. Moments
of self-centredness shocked him with their predictability. Almost forty and

the narration did not cease, the measured silken voice-over. Millions
of noncelebrities wishing they could star in a commercial, and

then the few thousand who'd actually had that opportunity, whose
grandchildren could be told, yes, Grandpa used to be on

TV, he was so gorgeous that a bigwig producer picked
him right out of a crowd one day as he

left the subway. A real standout. The ad was for
kitchen floor cleaner, groundbreakingly masculinist at that, about the multi-tasking

that a man of the new age (here we mean
the 'Zeroes' – that's what we used to call them) could

achieve by cleaning his floor while doing calisthenics, with washing
scours that attached to the bottom of his Contoured Men's

Nikes! He didn't want to leave the train. The children
would be in school until 3:30, and it was barely

lunchtime. He'd imagined all the passengers to be ending their
day, but it wasn't so; like him, they were working

at surviving the noon frenzy. From seven AM, when the
children woke him with shrieks of embattlement, the day's hours

had seemed to infinitely reproduce and expand themselves. And the
red sky? It had only been coloured toxins in the

air penetrated by the bold eye-of-God sun. The unshaven boy
may have just gotten himself out of bed, and his

dishevelment was the product of oversleep, not the kind of
exhaustion he might have endured as a university student bent

on originality. Up all night painting for an alcoholic has-been teacher
whose idea of great composition was the dissection and redistribution

of every element of the male form, coloured in great
swaths of pigment, textured, worked up, as though the surface

of a painting were a thought screen for a paranoid
schizophrenic, projecting that, as a young post-virginal man, he might

relate to the skewered body of this art, the hyperporousness
of self one felt being fucked over and over from

every possible angle by an experienced fucker's imagination. Really, these
were the sorts of conversations one could pay the university

in which to engage, and then in fatigued befuddlement at
four in the morning he would wander to the freight

elevator at the rear of the all-night garage of a
studio and see if the object of his obsessive interest

of the moment were there. And there she'd be, monkey-squatting
in one corner of the elevator, arms straight and swaying

from between her knees, completely looped on acid, staring glazedly
past him and drooling slightly, fulfilling his exalted idea of

a sexual messiah. It was months before he actually slept
with her, rolling onto a mattress that had dropped like

an oxygen tank from the far wall in her little
dorm room. She'd said with earnest and generous praise, now

you are the sort of boy who really should be
on birth control, lamenting the condom she'd been smart enough

to stick on him. He wouldn't have known how to
layer it on the moment, moving with the velocity of

a plunging plane to the sudden airbag, woozy with beer,
wine and cheap ouzo, poured over her homemade pasta casserole

and garlic bread – the measures she'd taken rather presciently thoughtful
the same way a kind uncle might plan a birthday

celebration. He'd left uninjured and rather head-floaty, as if the
pieces of desire-narration to anyone else in the future would

never completely make sense, yet he would never care for
that gap anywhere near so much as for the fact

of having been finally initiated, and decently. There, the obvious
untranslatability of all desire. Whosoever should be picked out as

anyone's love object must be distinctive from the norm, for
if the norm actually were stuffed with amorous charisma, we'd

all be in love with the same sap. Each of
us lands on the illuminated bulb of difference, and try

explaining it to your best friend. It's no easier than
making a convincing account for the senior relatives. There's no

real point in loving anyone beyond the claim to human
kinship, but love is what is done, with frequency, and

many times even with plausibly novel flourishes. No one on
the train had caused him to fall in love, however,

and he became sad at the thought that this new
crew proved that the average toss of the public dice

produced a plateful of single-digit disappointments. There were really not
that many attractive people, those for whom the norm was

warped to the specific angle he liked. One in a
few hundred, if that. And each of the truly attractive

ones was only so due to her or his charming
reminiscence of others he'd already admitted to loving in some

way in his past. They echoed something that had been
defined earlier on. They were not new. They were walking

memories the way dog owners air their dogs, looking sidelong in
the opposite direction when the pet begins to shit in

the middle of someone's garden, daydreaming like sailors, a cool
wind tossing their hair playfully over their eyes, and then

a tug to bring the darling animal, really exactly like
a winsome toddler, back into the fold of the sidewalk.

Then off they'd go. Sidewalks were spaces where he felt
safe. He liked the way they were built of squares,

some stamped with the date of their pouring, their smoothness.
The odd times when the children began chanting, as if

infected by faeries' slime, about stepping on the cracks and
breaking his back, he winced and reassured himself that children

must hate their fathers a little, or be careful not to hate
them too much, and that like every other secret this

hate would be immediately confessed, to the only person they
loved as much, their father! He had said it over

and over about his own father, wondering what the words
meant, really, what did they mean? It was a riddle

against sex, evidently, that trespassing the asshole would lead to
that back-breaker, murderous incubation, then delivery. They railed against their

own presence on the sidewalk as children born from their
father's pain. Who cared – it was a skipping song, one

that got them off at a good clip, marched them
flightily to school in a private competition that released him

from supervisory precision. As long as he could hear them
singing they were fine, like in the tub when he'd

gone to fold the laundry and instructed the littler ones
to keep their voices up. It was wrong not to

see them, but it was also wrong to sit lazily
observing them splash bathwater on the tiled wall and get

nothing done. He couldn't stand, most of all, getting nothing
done. There was one woman on the train now who

had forgotten to look away. Perhaps she was thinking of
something or someone, and not aware her gaze gave the

appearance of activity. He'd blinked downward, shy of reciprocal encounters,
embarrassed to be seen without his children, for here he

seemed moorless, jobless, thought-free, indolent. Who was he to be
riding about on the train? Where was he going? An

itinerary of destinations occurred to him, as if an urgent
e-mail had popped onto his screen, or a note was

passed to him by an underling at a tense moment
during a pivotal meeting with a client: the gym, a

movie, Metro Hall, a doctor's appointment, a focus group where
he would provide his opinion on a new mouthwash, a

date with a photographer. That was it, he was off
to meet his photographer. He was going to have his

picture taken naked. Not as a syrupy planned present for
his wife, not at all, but as an image bound

to be compared with his own polaroid-blue record of the
body he'd had as a twenty-year-old. He was supposed to

arrive by two, and, to suppress natural bloating, not to
have eaten for at least eighteen hours. The chocolate biscuits

he'd snuck making the older girl's lunch couldn't count, surely?
And the bulge below his chestline never left now anyway,

not even when he fasted for an important occasion, or
at the change of seasons. If he caught a bus

immediately from the platform, he might make it to the
glorified storage locker where Lucent worked, marked by a giant

lilac-coloured door, the kind that ripples upward like a magic
withdrawal of insecurities, a bold reconciliation of desire and self-denial.

If he missed the bus and took a cab, he'd
still get there but it would set him back an

extra twenty-odd bucks. Once you've committed to a thing, missing
it altogether, and for such a flimsy excuse as poor

timing, seems the greater sin. He would peel one of
the three twenties he tried to always keep in his

wallet, kiss it goodbye. You only live once. His clothes
would fall away. Lucent would place a glass of wine

and wink when it was permissable for him to let
it salve his dry throat, stinging a little as he

swallowed, and then he'd resettle his lips into the slightly
parted semi-smile he wanted to see himself make. Not one

of those boyish grins – bellhop grins, he called them. Ladder
climber grins. Mid-range family restaurant waiter grins. As if a

man is born to show his diffidence as a mere
aspect of intact masculinity. This portrait would be art-directed from

the inside out, and the evolution of his agency and
beauty would be self-explanatory when he held the proof alongside

the cloying photo of his first engagement party, 1984. He
deeply wanted there to be definable differences. At the age

of twenty-one, he had planned to marry. He had asked, in fact,
and been accepted, though not without drama. He and his

girlfriend had been in Mexico, at a roadside tortilla stand,
and he'd choked on some cheese going down sideways. He'd

choked chiefly because he was about to confess how he
didn't know if they were right together, but translated this

to its opposite, almost as if the words emerged, one
after the next, as the fluttering butterfly identity of all

good emotion, out of the nasty, dank, boring chrysalis of
rumination. Colours surrounded them, and after tracing out various ribbony

shades with her green eyes, she smiled broadly. On the
next bite he choked, and she hoisted herself on the

weight of one forearm and jerked upward under his ribs.
The wad of cheese flew out like a piece of

gum. He was unstuck; he was stuck in love and
the idea of a wedding he couldn't even imagine, not

being the kind of man who'd made his Ken dolls
marry or throw baby showers or any of that. On

the plane home, the cabin jolted and dropped, and a
steward fell into his now-fiancée's lap, one flapping hand flat

on her jeaned crotch, followed by the remainder of his
slender waist and hips and perfumed hair. How about you

marry him, he thought, you've got a career already, you've
seen the world. Me, I've seen the prairies, the burping

clam burrows of Cape Cod, my dorm. I've fucked two
women, what am I thinking? The steward scrambled upright and

opened and clenched his hand a few times, unsure of
how to politely thank her for her help while erasing

the embarrassment of inappropriate implication. As if mere contact were
a sign of will, choice, desire, destiny, aim, intent, consciousness.

All of the surrounding passengers caught it, and right there
and then he was able to hold the event against

her, to glaze it with other such indiscretions, to build
a case for the unsuitability of their plans now that ...

But really, it was the male student he slept with
who undid his marriage prospects. Call it a college fling,

a gender excursion, a reorientation, the image of his naked
body under and against another man's shimmered as though dipped

in love heroin. His senses came alive, he laughed instead
of sobbed after sex, he felt lifted and reformed. Not

that he stopped caring for the girlfriend. It was just
a verdict about the true and eventual package deal; he

wouldn't marry. She was surreally understanding, as if the idea
of the engagement, like a cake in the oven for

half its baking time, hadn't really set, had congealed only
about the edges. The moment of inflationary magic had not

occurred, where the trapped air puffs up inside globules of
batter and the whole concept lifts to its highest potential,

seals itself into that classically impressive form in which it
cools until it's eaten. So no one was really hurt,

he remembered, no one was defiled by his own flailing
attempts to know himself. Even he was never bitter about

the change of heart. What was the rush for everyone
to decide and measure and set down regulations for their

wants and whims? And why did he not feel the
same implicit obligation like a noose around his waist? The

rope tying him to the rest of poetry was a
ribbon wound in concentric hulas, and he'd learned to swing

it, loose and breeze-like. It kept winding its way around
him as he aged, up through the teenaged years, through

his twenties, through the thirties, still he was not tethered –
he was held, yes, but not stymied or leashed or

preregistered for a certain pattern of china or stemware or
silver cutlery. He was in the whorl of it. His

eventual wife did not expect much from their wedding day
beyond a manifesto of enduring mutual self-revelation; and he returned

this promise, and they kissed in front of everyone who
meant anything to them (except for Elevator-girl) and went nowhere

for anything like a honeymoon but settled down to have
their first child, a daughter who taught him to stay

up most of the night while still staying up all
of the day. He could tell his wife was troubled

by her deep identification with the girl, and he cajoled
her into viewing it as a natural confusion, more to

pacify his own shortage of such feelings. There she was,
a small squirming, sometimes-purple-faced human who could suck milk right

out of his wife's body and settle. He wished he
had the capacity to render another person subliminally, subcutaneously, full.

That the wife's body was slowly trickling down to become
the pillowy flesh of their baby … it was almost unbearable

to think of. He awoke shuddering some days, despairing for
the old days in the studio. Almost like a commercial

break, where the TV volume suddenly rises, the train squealed
into the next station. He'd missed his stop for Lucent,

and now that the choice was upon him, he felt
disinclined to spend even ten bucks on a cab anywhere

and instead transferred out of the burgundy-upholstered car onto
the platform. His knees ached a little against the shift

of activity. The kilt had been a poor choice, for
the wind still bit at the backs of his thighs,

pushing quills of cold up his spine and out along
the backs of his arms. His elbows were pulsing and

he squeezed them against his sides. He would walk out
of the station and slip off down along the ravine,

stumbling a little on the thick rubber heels that seemed
to swell the proper size of his feet, almost like

snowshoes for the tar sands. Then got his balance by
calling up the physical memory of navigating a balance beam,

when a youngster in junior gymnastics, of imagining a thread
dropping from the middle of his brain through the gall

bladder and due south through the perineum's span, then dangling
auspiciously between the stockinged moving calves. Give this thread a

pull and up his arms and legs would pike, like
a startled cartoon character! He laughed to himself, smelling fresh

new leaf growth, the fiddleheads unfurling to their feathery tips.
A mulch of fallen leaves and cedar twigs held early

morning rain and a squelch burped up with each step.
He watched his thighs move underneath him, like a metronome

carrying his torso into music. Ahead the river unspindled. A
few joggers gusted past, their sweaty smell hanging behind them

in the air, attaching to his hair and cheeks. He
instinctively stopped inhaling. He didn't admire the smell of strangers,

and felt himself to be unduly porous in a crowd,
as if the pall of people extended past their skins

and clothes and could adhere untidily to his own psyche,
tainting him somehow. He liked to remain separate. Soon the

woods felt quiet, and he stopped expecting another runner to
burst in on his solitude. From a young age he'd

craved this kind of moment, the sense of absolute privacy
in a natural setting, where he could simply breathe, amuse

himself with the beginnings of games and songs, where he
could speak out loud to imagined friends, conduct relationships of

import and magnitude, discuss why things must be as they
were, where he could use his pidgin French as if

a high-ranking diplomat sorting through the most privileged of receiving
lines. He hated the actual presence of others but loved

to imagine himself surrounded, hosting them all. He would think
of himself as a ball-gowned princess, even, or a thug,

running drugs and hoisting women onto beds in dank motels.
One image would move and float into another. Alone in

the woods he felt perhaps more comfortable and accompanied than
at any other time, regardless of the lover or friend

or relative he might have been with. Perhaps closest now
was his sense of peace when reading to his children

or watching them play their own games of magical intervention.
His wife had admitted being jealous a few days earlier:

Why can't you relax with me? Why must you leap
up from the couch like that, when I've only been

leaning against you watching a silly cop show? You spend
an hour with the children putting them off to sleep!

What is it you're trying to get away from? He
had blanched and lied, and she'd said, I can see

right through you, don't you realize? You're the worst liar!
He'd shaken his shoulders as if his hands were tied

and he needed to rid himself of a coat, or
perhaps it was as if he were trying to shimmy

like Houdini out of a straitjacket, the emergent thought like
a new raw shape of himself entering the room, until

there it was, the thought that he preferred being alone,
or with the kids, and what was so wrong or

unnatural about that? You don't see anything lacking? His wife
had turned to him with reddened cheeks and a half-open

mouth and exhaled as if simply frustrated past the point
of speech. He countered, Would you rather I didn't love

the kids as much? She began to nod her head
and press her lips into a grimace, There's just nowhere

to go with this conversation, I'm going to the basement.
What for, at this hour? To do some of my

own work, and see how you like being abandoned at
the best part of the evening, when we could actually

talk or – Or what? Is it that you want to
make love? – Oh sure, make it all so serious, I

was talking about TV and you turn it into sex,
every time. With that line, they'd burst apart, into opposite orbits,

and pretty soon each would breathe more easily, sensing the
plenitude of oxygen in each annex room. His chest would

puff up as though he were a duck about to
fling itself up into the sky, away from the shrill

surface of the river, its triangular feet inelegantly tucking back
and up into underfeathers, the wings stretching to either side

and lifting, lifting him like a football toward the clouds.
So what if the argument had been required to lift

off? Both felt freer in their separate space, he felt
sure the wife was happier there with some time to

herself after her long day at the office, a few
moments to putter about and put things in neat order

and sense the calm of the house now that the
children were safe and away and wouldn't be up again

for seven or eight hours. Ah, that time, whole like
a horizon, and even the ducks flapping far left above

the subway station and far right above the bulldozer pulling
up loads of garbage to expand the ravine did not

intercept any of the whooshing liberty of this moment for
him. The quiet and rapid ascent. As he crested a

breeze he thought about how the subway ride was frightfully
similar, how the solitude possible among other riders was perhaps

the next best thing to climbing to the centrepoint of
a bridge and staring beyond the trestle at the ground

below, the way trees looked like cabbages, how houses dotting
the landscape shone like home plates for an athletic hawk.

What did flying require, really, except the expectation of a
conscious descent? He turned his eyes from the distant ravine,

covered his ears against the gulls calling him to join
them in their anxious pack behaviour; he made his way

to the crosswalk at the east end of the bridge
and buttoned his collar as he walked scrupulously between white

lines leading to the far side, to the shops, to
a no-name drugstore. He would buy a box of condoms

now and slip it into his knapsack, then head south
to the rolling hills of the park. Surely there'd be

someone to fuck today. His scrotum ached for the right
press of an unknown human receptacle, craved the complicated sensory

mesh of entering and being entered, of flying and not
landing, of seeing from a high point what a ceiling

accurately looked like close-up. No doubt someone would open to
him. He would instruct his own prudery to take itself

for a walk down the path while he unmasked and
decorated his best features. The latex smell had a way

of jamming itself in his nose and he winced, Oh,
to have just the powdery flesh again in the mouth

without all the fear, all the tremulous and preparatory proxy.
But forget it! A thin envelope keeping him from the

world was consonant with all his habitual preferences, he wouldn't
fight it, especially if it meant keeping his family safe

from the aspects of privacy that were not private but
shared privately. His wife had her own world, he was

sure, the realm of the office where colleagues invited her
to lunch and delivered birthday greetings with more exuberance than

he and the children had mustered in their parallel stirrings
toward the school day, while foraging under the couches for

missing library books, in locating the matching rain boot and
hairbrush and slipping the nutritious lunch into each backpack. Their

cards were heartfelt and graphically splendid, yes, and his pancakes
were flawlessly studded with organic berries, their juice running navy

with heated sugar, and each had kissed her specifically on
her birthday forehead as if she were the daughter among

a quartet of adoring caregivers, and she had smiled forcelessly
and looked satisfied. Then left for the office, and he

with the children across the several blocks to school, with
the eldest sparkling powerfully at her ability to give pleasure

in the world and the younger ones humming and skipping.
Hardest about this preference for solitude was his unsurpassed desire

to give to others, without the usual conversation about decent
reciprocity. He'd rather, on virtually every occasion, simply give and

give and give. He became annoyed at how he was
expected to slide to the spectrum's opposite end and receive

and be grateful and charming instead of frantically but invisibly
exhausted at the strategic triumph of his provisions. He liked

best the guest who knew to say Thank you, and
thank you again, who skipped the What can I do

to pitch in? with full recognition that this one, odd,
parenthetical occasion required only surrender and sensuous presence. That on

almost every other occasion it would be exactly the reverse,
that they would be the planner and executor of every

detail of service and innovation. His wife had pulled him
aside, though, the previous year, to suggest he at least

feign interest in help from the other husbands, for they
were becoming offended and a little hurt, and this too

was part of a good host's responsibility, to allow the
most minor of assistance to be cast as gold-circle kindness.

Perhaps I should pin up names on a donor wall!
he'd snapped, and she'd hushed, No, everything's lovely, we all

appreciate you so much, do you think it's time to
bring in the cake? The sulphur of doused candles stung

his eyes; there was no place to look except the
crotch of the man approaching from calm's green foyer. He

opened his mouth and torqued his neck as though hanging
from a bungee cord. Clouds gathered like photographers, crackling and

nudging themselves into position. There was a slippage of the
man's thumb against the head of his cock, the fleet

bagging of the member, then the hot tube of the
foreign mouth suckling him in and out, drinking him to

the surface of himself.

SCHOOLED

Actual bodies suffering events of the people

LECTION

This is my new book.
This is of jouissance and I
half smile. You are some

one I like a lit
tle playing to lose pants fair
ly. Her middle fin

gers smell of the juice
before curtains tank. Canis
ters of news reach the

front and then on cer
tain days we absorb you. In
dividuals can

be made to stand for
itself, in an upright e
lection. For most of

the day they resist
flashlights and batons, reverb.
Rooms are potent moors

but the book I wrote
when you were old. You were a
fraid of the proba

ble oil in corners
and also to blow apart.
Craps is a game one

feels like if some rel
ish his reservations. Cig
arettes and torches

are so boats rarely
have heaters. Our nation pro
fessionally stands

showering themselves
too evenly. The food all like
to crook most palling

on deep-seated er
rors. You can see for yourself
is the duck I caught

blindfolded.

MATIN

On every sidewalk life is occurring
with such flattered crispness for Marina
She would respond to such accurate
phrase She can recognize her role
in embellishing ordinary records Every fat
girl who goes by is rare
All specific other people exercise diligence
Edged thighs also lack of arm
flab characterize most humans against fluffy
trees Foliate nature Designated matrices Marina
is every cursed chick with large
soft breasts One ponytail whisks Her
parents worked as technicians with Central
Telegraph dispatch at fancy time when
cords were plugged by hand Marina
would sit at every vast soundboard
deliberately switching several lines She'd cut
off strangers in each random manner
Her parents remained gentle with her
Once she fell in every well
also her knees were torn Marina
can bleed purple to bright orange

Fingers of one hand entangle others
as Marina eats each cheese sandwich
Crusts are pinched Her mother adores
her picky little eater Marina's mommy
kisses her cool thin blanched eartips
Marina always thanks family formally *Thanks
very much Mom* says she Susanna
nods her chin *Good offspring* Frederick
is usually already at work His
plate jangles under Marina's when she

slides it into shiny left-hand sink
She wipes her placemat Susanna nods
again *Take your apple* she reminds
Marina savours all signifiers Frederick hunkers
behind his desk during lunch Marina
so slim-waisted hovers baleful at taller
hall mirrors Her brother much too
old for any form of surveillance
but Marina wishes she could watch
him shampoo his dog Steinway Maurice
digs culverts on sheep farms irrigating
carrot fields If Marina could sing
his praises aloud she would yodel
besides but she cannot carry rounds
of tunes She titters rhythms counterside
Marina taps marches from every place
throat becomes gut Clucks old disco

Sidewalks release heat of each hot
noon Boys dressed in blue shirts
open buttons Every bald fellow checks
his digital camera humming quiet grins
almost Cheshire Many girls carry rigid
striped bags Marina meets her friend
for Evian Both are tardy Each
confabulates why More fat girls walk
with awkward propped-up wiggles Teresa looks
like each beauty in bleached white
sleeveless turtleneck with green earrings Marina's
nipples perk up In every city
taxis pass like chinooks Air stinks –
even young men wear woven hats

Frederick lost one cap per week
Susanna picked up extras at confectioneries
featuring Chinese imports Frederick would squeeze
her shoulder Marina prefers terse control
of each ponytail with its ka-thump
upon her nape She loves Teresa

WIND

If you can avoid talking about
body then do so now please,
inside or

       Outside building that failed or resisted
bear caught in scent o'own whiff,
fish understand in fathom-deep percussion

       Wheat – Stalking one's old lover who
mysteriously stopped loving, grew some earned
some dug

       Up imprint may be I liketa
think about absence athought how not
possible, roof of hope, ceiling

       Tiles flipped all some way to Manitoulin
Lessons one might find appropriate afew
years:

       Worms came out toes writhingly What
you talking about he said you

       Really know howta bring things down
you seriously know how taruin
most of

       Bridge part of heart crystalline edge
tubular objects flour bag at ground

       Level list orange zest root cellar
factor stench decayed radish kind olive

Mess hire crew for stranded sequence
Calypso good name for sloops or boats

Not girls! Think of kid's future! Pride
veneer stripped from movement what

Got left? Lousy boring complainers Babies
make better government elected or not

Blue arc – space between phone calls –
bandanna so tightround your tongue bleeds
sand, really

ALIVE

Altercation is a breath

If bodies hauled out or put to death
    in brutal fashion if one
Ate large bowl popcorn his supper dishes drowned
    metal sink I
Going to die like that I dignified I
    thoughtful empirical proud

Excuse for containment what would really make us
    happy new outlook arms legs
Unique counting guests we have fifteen mouths bring
    me napkins feed him diuretic
Easily love read they find signs on major
    city streets beautiful they see

Worth dying part what you wearing to concert
    can't find anyone
Long one street madhouse circus carnival most people
    enjoy walk after
Lock forget it can't hear what you saying
    thought her waist was smaller

Senses sky's slow movement orange to black tinged
    moonlight regarding television we
Could not find cleaner zone I reading about
    in magazines no way
Children came out innards covered in blood body
    is tired

Can only be reattached if time on side
        what makes one person vomit is
You know six-year-olds they spell out
        whole alphabets with spines they cry so
Into your stomach many claim to be psychic
        how do we know if to be born

In grey pit let me leave your mind
        to rest for day has been
Rich food most friendships end after few years
        who has combination to my bike
But really not easy getting used to being
        keeps you quite sonic

LEASE

Impatient: You had visited the day of purchase,
Dates each had costumed. Every item on own

Hanger recalled the fabric, as I pushed each
Room, was emptied; then began the disavowal passing

My skin, on sculptural trays. Blouses skidded past
Years. Here was all my stuff, held through

The world until the glass vases. Dozens of
Objects I'd worn against it had been six

Matched earrings arrayed once or twice but
I, I used to live there. The room

On a scallop shell was filled with beautiful
Storage for today, and then: I left for good.

PHOTO

Extraconjugal moisture on sadness accumulated
from falling water, of photographs, taken

by rumours, which telling eradicated dawn
to bright midnight to dawn again – off-ramps.

The hot tendril (sic) we obscure, our willing
shuttered lens against evident processes

redirects still-sad chemicals with sweat
(I told you). I *told* you. Highway lights

hold dazed arms more or less as children
playing monster. It does not mean I can

see you. It is of its own sad developing.
On holiday I will make a technology,

promise. The lake: silvered thing. Dirt road
then rain. My contrary nature (nay,

sure). Time biding with ridiculous dearth
of practice (four times over from a letter

sadly flirtatious, trying to be glad or tender,
dinted, reticent; various gists of depiction).

THE LOVELY FIGURE

Kiss you on the cheeks, that double-round coital zone, the lovely figure
I have loved over and over

In a dream of you, the lover who comes and lifts
eyes from the trouble of me.

Mirage, I know you're a poor fuck; what I want
is the light, the light, to wake

To a tray of eggs and coffee, newspaper
with a good review and the cuckoo-sound of children

Eating in the kitchen, my empire clamouring
with good clocks.

PRESENT

Did you think about that other future,
the one you might have bought into
when stocks were safe? Can't
be bothered, I'm off
for booze and smoked cheese
and we will have a party

We will see a new year's cumulus
burst to flower!

Punctual soldiers, well, they're ill-accounted, reverse-
furloughed

Telephone poles mark a street's dodderish length

Sky presses past. One thing:

Don't strap yourself in, unless the car's
motion tells you *Ah the guests*,

they're here

FREED

Lasting	thought
It morning again so	sky
Painting exhibition of new irksome	vantages
What's	lunch
Hit again with da big	money
Balcony alchemy: suggestion: recurring dream: appended fear:	death
Cascaded giggles in	foyer
Da skin dat you feel 'suits'	me
Turn lights to feral	periphery
Sure, snore	now
I luft	*you*

CURE

A brain holds you in space the way mine did once. That best
friend of desire, and what you feel
you might think if thinking
could hold you.

How do you know the weather has tipped from normal
to absent, aberrant, importunate
if the weather resembles an inning
of baseball ended, and where is the hot dog vendor
and where are pickles among the cart's
many orificious freebies?

You don't know what you think or feel. You only
think and feel you know, and wave from the window
and think of something else to eat
for the sun is disappearing at the western dip
between the houses onto which you look
when you stare into the road beyond it
trying to recall a word for cooking steak
in a flash, in a pan.

Pardon me if I think I know the only
cure for you is love that will not quit
the premise of its origins.

AN HONEST OFFER

Perhaps thought does what it's supposed
to do, humiliate the thinker
into moving toward a new one.

The last flaming thought *flames*.
The last shaming thought *shames*.

Rhyme, rhythm. Time, plosion.
Why stop there?
How did the final thought know
what it would think, like her father
and her father before him
and her father ...

I wouldn't shoot empty flak at thought. But that's just me.
Nails strapped around a girl's chest
shocked and charred at least one large last thought.

Berserk fire sideways as rain,
and the blood inside that
black in the dot screen – schemed lines –
the first blaming
taught the same shame.

The overall rhyme seems corrupt
only when you think it throughout
the deftness of memory (**bang**) instead of
the deafness of action (**pow**). Except

'have no thought' is not an honest offer, is it?
'Shot by shock' seems redundant but may not be.
Already some are deafening a way
out of the market. Good idea:

there is an exploded leg on the sidewalk
in the Reuters picture
of the sidewalk. A human foot
berserkly apart, its unwrecked shin

above that, black fringe of smattered blood

you think
above that. (See, thinking did not stop.)
A shard shorn of body, charred.
An effect blown out of portions.

Troublesome moiré: shocked shot.
Come on, blame the paper or me for all these bad times
and the chest before that, wrapped –
and the scheme before that, plosive –

and the first thoughts,
whose regrettably undeaf thinking was enough
to stop rhyme from making an honest offer
and an honest offer before title

and an honest offer before shame before
the berserkly frontal
FUCK YOU
of a flame.

(No, I won't think about that, won't
think what I thought just then,
just now.)

THE PROBLEM

Official details of *The Problem*

– *We were both very angry at each Other Each of us was The two*

– *Of the both of the couple of Us were equally making strange with the*

– *Other We were estranged in tandem One Believed the second was wrong and so*

– *Did the first Every moment passed like Its inverse memory Each colour flashed its*

– *Complements I thought you could behave better And you said I conducted myself with*

– *Impunity We did not desist or cease Each inserted tension There was no space*

– *Between the breath each took to gird The gut for the next round We*

– *Were both ready for anything it took And it took years just to bat*

– *An eye at exactly the same time Neither of us reared up toward sympathy*

– *The twosome was loathsome which each levered To similar advantage We were one in*

– *Our hatred We were together in shared Honest grievance from the heart and head*

– *And how it hurt so Each felt it Both felt us We*

Formal arraignment of *The Items*

1   We were both very angry with each
    Did black first Every moment passed like
    Both felt All traded an eye for
    Neither of us reared white toward sympathy

2   And how it hurt so Both felt it
    An eye at exactly the same time
    Its inverse memory Each colour flashed its
    Darkest night Each of us was the two

3   Complements. I thought you could behave better
    Of the both of the coupling of
    Honest grievance from the heart and head
    And it took years just to batten

4   Our hatred. We were together in our
    Us were equally making strange with red
    And you said I conducted myself poorly
    Were both green for anything it took

5   Tough gut for the next round We
    To similar advantage All were one in
    Another Double estranged in dual tandem One
    Impunity We did not cease and desist

6   Every twosome some loathsome which each levered
    Between purple breath all took to gird
    Believed the second was wrong and so
    Yellow inserted tension There was no space

One specific salient *Item*

that's where you're very wrong
there IS no space
no space on earth big enough so kindly
shut the door on your
way out thanks

Ten helpful and succinct *Talking Points*

10   For openers, shut up and blow

9   Blue sky, orange water it's called Shut up Sunset

8   That's what I was saying There's no

7   Go Blow Sunrise that's bigger than the both of us

6   There's no bloody us on the horizon go blow yourself

5   U is for Up, S is for Shut as in

4   Losers are who you make shut up

3   Over the rainbow sucks Blow the rainbow will ya

2   Will has not a lot to do with it out on the abandoned corn fields
     of Kansas, the flaming oil fields of Kirkuk

1   Will is the spoil, but IYKWGFU* don't talk about that

*if you know what's good for us

GRIEF

And if this is the beginning

you know how you got here

My heart is about as big

as a car It goes fucking

nowhere I had a habit of

telling so much people wanted to

say pass the salad Over in

a ghetto there are actual people

suffering events of the body Thing

about a hand is you can

give it a shake and shove

it Moreover I have a full

life of the first order So

many little griefs it is pointless

to make out the distance of

the present Sugar Driver tells me

all about how he's the only

one to clean the inside of

his cab I believe him from

the back seat it is spotless

I was going fucking somewhere if

I could get there in a timely

manner He gassed on the step

I farted lightly Sorry I said

It's pretty damn clean in this

damn cab Walking is always better

idea Grief is grief at least

at your feet Grief will burn

us all up if we let

its little horsecurl flail Heart palpitations

start and stop and ache and

stripe my chest I am patterned

Breath is an altercation Give it

up baby give it forth Heave

off for the sake of the breasts

you can still carry

EXPLAINING LANDSCAPE PAINTING TO
THE ACTIVIST

For rivers or fields
we ride over, russet harvest,
terse and stern humans
on a train. All are arriving
somewhere.

Do you think you are aware of trees?

Hmm, flock swoop. Swamp
stealth tethers horizon level.
Canadian nature looks pretty good, pretty, good.
Her cellphone rings, plays terrible
Led Zeppelin. Freight tug ahead
causes us miserably to slow and it is even
raining. Red-breasted birds like ideas
of ideas.
Are.

To witness a stasis
simmering seasonal blood and body
of near-wild's measure. Correction, surely.
You can see it clear out a large window:
Smashed-flat Chevrolets piled by the blue spruce
ready to be trunked for living rooms
in December.
                    Bicameral
vista, lime-lovely this side compared to
stunning orange that. Fruitful step-
bridge of plain vision, on which one regards:

        The painter, out there, carmine
        robes ermine collar, with palette
        in the drizzle doing commissioned portraiture

of the pasturelands. White
no black heifer. Beige
sheep. Mimicry
of cloud cover. And,

okay, we half-wonder what a family
feels of master's impassioned absence,
this portly record-dabbing –
Will art last longer for example
than plastic pterodactyls from Vietnam?
Distinct, is a probability.
Consenting.
And by the way, with your coffee,
     shall
invasions be permitted to
exterminate rogue tyrants overseas
who behoove all subjects to recline
a certain perfect panorama
of surrender, of bleached-thin civilians
with political limbs axed, hung to dessicate in the sun
for billy clubs, question mark.
       Aw twist
shut your tubes of watercolour, divvy
canned beans in the soup kitchen.
Weigh lichen.
    Nose to face
furrowed lands we have made, each kilometre
gobbled by snores to the stately
station.
Termina,
us.

*

Personal belongings claimed.
Aisle jammed with keen exiters. For the road,
                    how 'bout just an
estimate: do
          you believe, feel, imagine,
          think you are, sort of,
timid? Well, that's a portion of it, too much
comfort perhaps – crossed with vigour. Now we're again
possibly chatting, enchanted by recollected autumn, how every leaf
chirruped red breast and its plate-glassed dressage
of golden colour. I get it now.
Ah –
it's beauteous and poem-like –

so very Alive, like

each of us
in our opinions. So
what old growth can we possibly ruin
with our conversation?

SCHOOL

Foreword

In her jewels an enigma reflects most often 'I want
to go home' Admiration is not demented even after centuries

After all the copies drawings engravings this body of work
toward a labour of the beautiful gives me a taste

for the epoch that we know so well.

The First School

'Treasure of marvels' a retreat of her image The art
of living by luxury and the ideals of impossible pleasure

We have royal hands Fluctuating and indecisive art offers to
our eyes all its most exterior fruits In the age

of the grand rhetoricians lyrical songs after the sinister business
renounce to borrowed charms by an overly large familiarity with

conscience and the classes at the heart of this fever
And maybe artists speak of almost nothing jealous of the

worse suppositions and refinements of the spirit Is it jealousy
toward 'strangers'? Between the impression of a brusque rupture and

the voyage of the ideal does language in reality have
the taste deliberately turned toward a search singularly modern? We

77

researched the rarity of the subject aroundabout Proportions of an
unconscienable coquetry Art of a fashion Even more and smiling

Her drawings showed us the unknown for the first time
The seductive originality of compositions Of exchanges that imply an

intimate collaboration Some figures emerge little by little from anonymity
It is impossible here even to refer to them The

current master of taste does not disappear to the death
of her most famous symbols She is known by the

bag of the city which gives her privileges and liberty
Independent whole violent erudite cerebral refined at the middle of

a pure illusionism To whom comes the idea of this
union? Her strange rotations mentioned among the artists read themselves

then respond to scenes of apparent estrangement in which the
frame of the senses is reinforced Which salamander runs each

of these grand tableaux under the direction of her artist-boss
of a smiling nostalgia and holes the least clear We

see the dryness to which is joined lucidity Each view
wears this injury-mask of the century to its own tinted

interrogation But the spatial problem has left her senses almost
surrealist Her figures isolated from the masquerade uncomforted haggard

surely the most interesting of this ensemble We know almost
nothing of these same symbols held in the manner of

an exploited section for some terms of framing such that
the views are often empty and inexpressive We have changed

the style of purism which fucks with the academy Her
works are not well known yet are in place which

is an intimate fusion A good example of short eclipses
of the particulars which are the origin of our style

(hell!) She shows how to imagine the seduction which expresses
all susceptible poetry 'If I had found others who could

have made work as good as hers I would not
have bothered her but there was no one so capable No one'

Nature is for her the sensuality of the subjects and
her so-spontaneous touch We know of her a sensitive writing

without a doubt to complete an unfinished set-up of a
chromatic fantasy Naturally All of it These familiar landscapes are

brought to life in little scenes This lost composition is
not isolated A work this personal has been greatly admired.

A Section

We know
         that she has illustrated numerous works
                                  with a
vehemence both
         flexible and light This lucidity will
                                  not permit
her role
         as decoder of the symbols of
                                  the blue
fountain But
         the echo pierces any evident single-mindedness
                                  Elegant A
certain left-handed
         zeal is used to express horror
                                  This is
the work
         of a personality of a sensitivity
                                  with a
difference Visibly
         perhaps placed on the page captured
                                  in a
drawing The
         litany of personae colours catches you
                                  by surprise
Near these
         almost undiscussable canvases rests the critique
                                  of style
of which
         we know still
                                  almost nothing.

The Second School

In this second school of
which we know almost nothing
little seems to have the
temperament of a boss exaggerating

musculature so sensitive with a
paradoxical virtuosity between the windows
or sacred The ambitious decoration
through the first school must

not forget feelings gone excessive
Taste changes Like fashion having
carried the best of a
style Of a culture ...

RICHARD IS RELEASED

Orphans morph onto orchards
Parents of waifs aim for a Waldorf school
Lost toddlers stammer a little
Extroverts tie their shoes together
Widow is a window what did I tell you
Wife for life
Austere like Austen
Maximum security prison is most safe
Talented hosts offer crackers not tuna
Children trip on the buddy system
It's systemic claim three advocates making one point after another
Laws yearn for breakers I mean bricks
Mourners over a plot
Coven of each to her own haven
Those leaving veer back to Montessori, friendly like
This place is crawling with teachers she retorted
Mix me a cosmopolitan or a Pink Lady
Front seats reserved after for Carmen
Dress up pleaser punks trash walls oh putty pleaser
That's lewd not popular
Knickers not suitable for kindergarteners
Who died anyone I know
Richard's parents purse cracked lips
Not this orchard it's moister plus more obvious
Loudspeakers keep spewing loud shit
Loud speaker keeps spewing what did you say
One or both took a shit together in the same cell blockage
Husband nabs remote folds paper names witness nukes leftover chokes snoring
Wakes up gasping
Introversion

Little one in flames
Little one in empty space
Little one in locked box tied down
Two to a booth soft orifices
Open window is a widow did you forget to tell me
Lifelong buddies untethered
Untethered
Crisp ashes in the right orchard
Richard morphs fire to poplar
Pieces of Dicky wind up on a pleasant breeze
Several mourners stammer minimal
Sincerity then hunger for crackers
Like every orphan in a meadow
Listening to opera through solo window of a widow
Turns up speakers on a low sill airs out
Bitter tuna odour haven of each
Haven of each
Richard is released

BOOK

(WHICH READS YOU ALOUD)

The cab of his inside

Evening tore itself apart at thought that it
should be just nother regular kind when children

                              screen time er parents dish doozies er sky
                              rolls coal dark er then it as not day That chronology

effin evening tore self to pieces Waves crashed upon
cement dock Cars pitched past white double line such

                              pedestrians rushed verge green light they'd waited
                              patient as pink citizens tending war will won't precur Yer

hopes are unreliable Yar dreams are mildewed by improbable
symbolism er deferred Toyotas At three in mahning

                              streets are vacuumed er yet civilization as at its most
                    complimentary Streetlamps curtsy Raccoons stockbroker in back lane

rootish er salivating for more effin discarded styrotrays panned
with poultry juice Synthetic surfaces command attention effin tall

                    aromatic organisms Cozy sheets flannel sleepers Snow er night
                    are three favourite camouflages Flamboyant flames effin your collie-dog

flower length effin sheer torso thus hug you Who
fumed enough faction in your teens er twenties to carry

                    you through consensual production code effin present Don't
                    know what party as If recess comes sooner because

seasons are moving then who am I to desist
with irksome cushion envy Something pulsive in backyard left

     prints er grey scat Wires bowed er bowed Mulishly polite's synecdoche
          at rest when world sword wants to make rash crash wretched

er crass terrific vent front event on newspaper
er splatter us Population as safe weird are safe weaker

       safe embedded in all-new-material duvet Oh several virtued clean
      cervical caps who washed cunts jasmine-doused soupçon effin seabreeze

Yikes armpits effin citrus milk-plump skin effin children
knapsacked for school with yogourt-packed tummies Dry ice

          edits sidewalks Our stagelights merger us our hoods er
        mitts er scarves buffer some who reboot god er Sun beams down

on go-to-war flavour effin twice-brewed coffee broth import
lounge interior caramel wainscotting across from homeless women's

       drop-in centre You forewarned clothes er toys ornery well-used but
      still-useful frypans er also varieties of canned goo versatile even

when unheated Thank you thank user no thank ugh for
oozed kindness Night should've been here again soon one justice

        has to subsidize to sixty about four hundred more referenda
       er click keyboards together *Voici voilà* I knew I could

spew if I really gave it my escape code Generosity
effin election as applied to those untarrying platforms whose natural beauty

        has deblinkered Hey dusk my camaraderie simplifies soon into
        pleats of my waist er salve me from overeating Restraint

as tenor effin enthusiastic dispensation Campaign makes one
swallow to read expansive than expected er then someone as

        classification to morgue to stethoscope loved one You
        never spoon dead er dying er living er unborn

but schmooze praise for contrite oceans to suture armies
Vote please er vote flat Asses shimmy clutter in sequined

        sequench You know what I mine You who know I
        mean what mine stay in heat er throttle effin

good car pool fill'er south fill'er east please with preteens and texts
er for religious specificity don't disinherit toque on

        hooligan again Pay me formica thoughts effin hue er
        hue er hue er hue er hue er blanded family

about whom I can care for only so many things
at win some loose some Have messy Calendar slows into sufficient as

        if summaries er memories swoon fickle gyrating gnome-structure er huff
        as fourteen snoring entity Middling classes Happy to

metre you in yard time effin desperate leisure-for-profit gains
Convivial vocals flit darkness as thirsty students on Ecstasy goosewalk

                    Main Street delivering themselves from studying studying what it
                    makes manly to enlist seriously when one grows no phat

Knowledge Provider Lady er would you have eensy baby
as I cannot Thank how very much Thank how extreme

                              such Let me smooch You are adurable I'll just
            depilate lipstick There peach-lite grope float Universal-Creator-Effin-All

knows er er er er er er er er
what will happen next but me have ~~poor poor~~ poor feeling

RUDDER

Was going fucking somewhere

UNCERTAIN INSTINCTS

silence: it's distributing
how one hears or a censor
at work. her senses say

shush up about it, or see
how certainty, so ebullient, hears one
seeing her. nonsense censors

work about it, shush sense
or up at certainty. say, even turbines
it's tributing: and such silence.

TEN CONCENTRATED TENETS ON
TERMS OF RENTAL

Centre yourself, concentrate or be stern,
earnest, and eventually seven rude tenants
select eviction naturally

Concentric turn-ons lathe, not lather, your
or my arousal and several secret yet common
resources earn a newer wad

Juice is a down-pressed concentrate
all natural, runs to your wrists and touch
touché, shush up about my hair or loss
is so distracting

Centre yourself leeward, in conviction, virtue
out of rudeness, must concentrate factually rather
than straight, ahead, align your yes
eyes with wider doors of lines

If you rent eccentric grammar shape up
or contract a little curl in your muddle around
which we will merger terms and rental tenets

Ear rims arouse lather to me and other
concentrated earners

Lychee

Rum-runnelled rubby elects
turnkey retraction over addled eked-out
panels for electric heat or softer hot water (This
is untruthful)

Stern nature cannot concentrate on only
you for you are you are you are you or hotter
we are not so central nor earnestly
aroused in secrets (This is truthful)

Several need other as near resources.

Run to my wrists now touché and
touch me centre or curl your fingers on me
contract a waddle concentrate and so
is loss distracting
So concentrate waddle centre
me to run several secrets
Now central you are for
you cannot nature softer
and eked-out addled turnkey
elects rum lychee
Concentrated other arouse rims
or terms which around curl
little shape grammar of lines

Align ahead factually

Concentrate out virtue leeward
yourself distracting
so about up and wrists
all concentrate juice wad
Resources common several or
later not concentric naturally
Select tenants eventually and
or concentrate
centre

THREE KINDS OF LABOUR

Quick! She only has a week or two, and
Down the chain of labour she descends, to
Guard her lover on the sidelines. Concentrates
Taut now. Leans in toward her shoulder – weighted
And burdensome as love is – she won't lie.

Love is heavy against time, heaves alphabetic
Loads of asphalt disordered by poets betting
Metaphysical labour. Heart rate melodium
Superior to overtime bonus. One better hard hat.
Cupid-cute decals, foam liners cushioning her eartips.

But there's this week, that's all, a lover's ultimatum.
Tired of the margins, mawkish re: boss's approval,
Pissed about the wait. She wonders which to labour
Gutterside – beloved's grateful kisses, or Game Cube
On a suede-screen home theatre. What'll keep her warmer?

SOONER

Sooner, we would rather

A sure, blesser wall

Over, all the terrible Edit Save

I'm postponing one jean crease

Father, you swell allowance

Rather, we thought sooner

Terrible and tacky as putty

Later, you have thought about it Edit Save

Upon my night watch, sneezer

Junior, paste will letter

We rather thought, sooner.

Sooner sensible censor centaur Edit Save enter.

Disturb turbine stern earnings early flyer.

Shusher Edit Save whisker rustic sticky putty.

This kind of obvious thing. Terrib.

Or is it evident? Other creasely thighs that distance.

Tucks under cover uncertain entries.

Entire body hush entire hush Edit Save hush.

My instinct is to jeans in cold weather.

Sooner is loot for later.

Aloof finger loofah makes for good swell, techy

I know, true Edit Save ruin truer.

Sleeter on the white notch regarding urban comeuppance.

Shut lunchtimer, we would rather.

Underwear.

Lessener.

Half the man on one hand. Wuh.

Hurt throat croaker Edit Save like a weekly fiver.

What sort of shirt in court is proper for a shy centaur?

Something sheer or fur? This soft of linen.

Certain instincts for cashmere flaws.

Breastless.

Speaking of, Edit Save been ages. Aegis.

Rather, we would sooner.

Edit.

Save.

Lighter

Under a dark soon, the stars rise.

Centaur

Such roars all evening, a bit confused.

Curtain

Behind watch, the specific passes to come.

This

Kind

Of

Bull.

Shush up about it.

Salad the pass. Push

Your rudder

Further.

CONNOTATIONS (OVERLAND VERSION)

how he she you can hear it all and what it was someone said
if as literally into some chest severe secrets note each mouth
over by the telephone made palpable

are impressions if for over by the telephone all
the soup fell into the shape of bowls mouthing
off at the first arsehole to join a manifesto

made palpable it's worthy of specific recall in corrosion
each anticipates personal sniping and jeered or cheaply formed
collapsibilities once grafted at the idea of being ill

chest collapsing just like that
fessed tune connoted
manifesto-like
he she my finale
get it
gut it
jest of howls
shape of jeers
literal earholes in exaggerated recall
concentrated
taut
shush up about it
is so distributing
say his her your senses palpable
on the telephone

ON BECKETT'S *PLAY* VIA MINGHELLA (DOWNLOAD)

Moor is a room overcrowded with caskets
Cadavers speak coldly when skinflesh cankers
How dare you love who you lover if you love
Grey surfaces surface from urns
Organ of the heart putrefies out human cheek cell by cell
Boils over Really over all of it
All of it worn on your faces
Feces
Of love
Moor is a room overcrowded with caskets
Cadavers speak coldly when skinflesh cankers
How dare you love who you lover if you love
Grey surfaces surface from urns
Organ of the heart putrefies out human cheek cell by cell
Boils over Really over all of it
All of it worn on your faces
Feces
Of love
Moor is a room overcrowded with caskets
Cadavers speak coldly when skinflesh cankers
How dare you love who you lover if you love
Grey surfaces surface from urns
Organ of the heart putrefies out human cheek cell by cell
Boils over Really over all of it
All of it worn on your faces
Feces
Of love

AN OPEN EROTICS OF GZOWSKI

The voice of   the bodiless lover   is a trope
for the world's   brooding power to   scintillate our aliveness

in physical space   To animate us   to our own
skin's porous interest   in exchanging matter   with the matter

both inside and   beyond its seal   The voice's perfume
crosses the bleak   dark valley we   like to consider

the separateness of   the individual; it   lets us be
in the midst   of an erotic   thrall while we

rinse our mugs   and wipe our   stained cupboards It
assures us the   body is not   a married organ

properly bound to   one dock but   a canoe, okay,
careening on a   fluid carpet of   whimsy and longing

virtually upended in   a spray of   language, seriously amorous
about the sea world   and all the   voices its sheathlike

structure would and   *can* contain

FILTERLESS (SOFT VERSION)

grid stripped
from the sensor's caution

excitement of touch concentrated
rose as dragonfruit

waxen surface which ships unsecure
what you shush yourself to

and topples fingers to catch
breath upon nipples

distributing possibility to rise or
suggest aroused ideas

toward dawn the light sifts, levers
a bird

cars motion exterior hours

glee of juices on the inner thigh

glee of rapid fluting in the mouths

circular escarpment of hip lines
certain against sunmesh

did you realize the muscular internet was modern?

did you cross-reference a messy palette of yearning?

was adjustment a token message
compensating for loneliness?

alter my angled knees
so your ass is a turbine

diligence in the digits

minor hairs rise as if baking

your smell is attractive

(I leaven you)

and the morning appears to be deciduous
with orange finery
and tender departure

THE GROIN AREA (WET VERSION)

Tender repartee taunts
if in a cockle is your conch
gush up mister
and who you desire might shelter peril
Minstrels tinker in arousal
teasing recent accounts
Finer surfaces elucidate serious
tact of required or vivid
acts of unskeined touch
Vivisect me with which-shaped gender
Bivalve us close by some mollusc
If in a cunt is your cock
slush up the foyer: ungroin
tubular organs as vital premonitions
Summon hands or fists even
to lush recesses
If us mean what some know
If I near who you keen
whether sister is an alias signatory
Reparate urges which undulate off-kilter
Bend and shimmer magnolia bladder
crepuscular asshole
Certain serious tacticians
of silence unskin who from whom
Emanate uncertainty and usher
up about its enigma
Name us on or in
Name us on and in
Cuck and a cont
Font and a fuck
Semi-intelligible insignia
by Anon will eventuate designation
If some or every know what

us mean when we intercept gossip
It's distributing exact practices
re: amorous pulsation
What some later call when it started
The groin area wetter to roam
repartee still and tender
such minstrel speech –
shush shush hush
about get else gush on lever us
with several words of advice
Gender us
gentle shelter overhead:
pear-shaped bulb a pulse
or else no lesser

RETREAT DIARY

First order of the full life

1   If birdchatter could not stir in her/him a familiar agitation, then the train,
barrelling from the southeast, could; he/she noticed the cabin's foundation
vibrating and the wicker chair she/he sat in almost emit a ringing sound.
The tracks all along the north shore of the lake began to roar, an
oncoming army bearing down on all efforts to relax. But to the left, out
the porch window an entire glass-topped lake sat, and held its own, and
the train gradually diminished in its ominous agency; technology would
pass on and he/she would remain here in the quiet evening light, its orange
brightness and effervescent spirit balancing a long firm note of permanence
against the always moving chicory-green fronds, lime-hued birch leaves
and self-proud pine nadirs. O the colour all around was joystruck or
caused her/him to become so, and he/she dropped plans of returning ever
again to the city where she/he had recently plunged from an acquaintance's
fourth-floor window to the purple tarp-reinforced canopy that gussied up
the condo's front turnaround. For whatever reasons, he/she'd landed in a
collapsible arabesque, the right knee sponging on impact, her/his two
palms crushed against a curvaceous metal brace which had caused the
perpendicular arc of his/her whole spine to ricochet backward and her/his
arms to stretch to the rear like wings on either side of his/her shocked face.
It was the backlash confidence of a novice Olympian who wobbles then
smiles a pure grimace on completion of an otherwise near-perfect floor
routine. Several pedestrians looked up upon hearing a shriek erupt in the
sky and then observed the flamboyant death drop and ridiculously
moderated ballet of deferred death. She/he went in an ambulance –
a wailing, winding one staffed by three overtired attendants each
outbutching his/her workmates – and the nurses tsked and chirruped at
her/him about how this run of bad luck could not be counted on in the
future and hadn't he/she better get her/himself straightened out, for the
child needed him/her; didn't she/he believe in how hinged he/she was to
the civic world? She/he told them all to shut the hell up and that it was none
of anyone's business, least of all theirs. They released him/her with wide
white bandages cuffing both sets of fingers, almost like restraint devices
for someone hooked on fist-fucking, which she/he wasn't generally but

could well imagine having been if Constantinople had opened to him/her in the way she/he'd wanted. Constantinople: the name burned in his/her gut and she/he swallowed all images away and imagined shitting them out strand by slimy strand.

Boats roared around on the lake; a burnished late-day sun gathered at the horizon and everyone on the water tossed their hair in the breeze; it was a divine night for feeling wind hit you in the breastbone and arrow its way through to your throat making you ululate like a Canada goose with a dozen honking buddies along to guard against nightfall's loneliness. Wherever would he/she be then? Where would her/his daughter/son, almost eighteen in another country, with faux-soie skin and connect-the-dot body piercings, Where? Ah, it didn't matter or its weight could never be measured by any scale that made sense to anyone else on the planet. He/she couldn't spare thoughts like this, had to preserve a focus on near-hopes and neighbouring attainables.

A distant motorcycle gunned its engine to the max droning about how a human life could singe a fireline right through any official paved surface and resurrect itself as a glitteringly regal dragonfly. Portals present themselves to the average person daily if transcendant awareness meshes with the right religious preconditioning, but she/he had forgotten all about that with his/her own education and certainly did not ache about the lapse of such branding within her/his son/daughter's. The baby believed only in food and its handy, hardy, ever-miraculous insta-provision. Hopefully the family she/he'd been carried off to, squalling in his/her little yellow-trimmed blankie, worshipped at the same altar. Hopefully the infant had been fed, all these years, each day, all the meals that make up a sensible vitamin-enhanced life in modern North America.

Loons pilfered the dusk as if they were strangling their young. She/he loosened his/her bra/jockstrap and unhooked the hooks and elastic that had been poking her/him in the middle of his/her spine/butt, then ran her/his hands to the front over each smooth bulge in turn, feeling the nipples' rubbery nubs and thighs' soft mounds edged by curling hair and moving upward to the strung mammalian tendons of his/her neck.

2   Across the matte grey water there sat the dingy brick hospital where she/he'd been born, its lone tall smokestack jutting into an equally matte grey sky, flanked on either expanse by puffy irregular deciduous tree-heads. Below the large ruddy rectangular conglomerate to the left, from his/her vantage sitting on the porch bed, glinted the muted turquoise dome of a pink gazebo, positioned on a rounded rockbank overlooking the far shore.

In that gazebo on one of its slivery perimetrical benches she/he had writhed against and tugged toward him/her the flanging muscles of several lovers' backs. She/he could still easily recreate the various torsos under his/her hands, each one with its differently laboriously exposed skin (this process of mutual unpackaging taking twenty minutes or an hour depending on the lover's courtship habits, natural patience and phobia of sex in public places, even if midnight on a semi-clement March or April night where it was unlikely strangers would materialize out of the dark at one of the gazebo's rotunda ledges), and he/she could feel the pair of bracing thighs squeezing her/his own, the naked feet clawing at the bench trying to preserve poise and hold off the body's craving for full-out sex – but this never happened in such places, not when he/she was a teenager. One such night she/he'd taken charge of his/her own capacity to produce pleasure in a lover (first simmer-over-and-gulp oral) and witnessed the escalation of her/his interior ladder of daring, the same lighting technician's ladder he/she'd clambered like a black-clad cat burglar up the slippery side of the amphitheatre after her/his brunette submissive Ricardo/Carmela's billowed-out orgasm, and tummy-hoisted her/himself onto the roof, crouching then standing to take large star-steps, and waved at him/her with her/his zipper open still, prostrate and white as a sheet in the gazebo, his/her face puzzling out, Who was this chick/guy? Ah, Carmela/Ricardo's nice kind of cock/cunt, and the beauteous colour turquoise.

The squawks and caws of ravens shot through his/her consciousness, and the peeps and squeals of flickers and jays and swallows. An almost-deafening pulsation of cricket song necklaced the morning, and she/he could imagine diving into the crisp water and yanking its cool volumes with his/her hands and pushing her/his own here-streamlined, here-burbled bulk forward in viscous surreal underwater space and time. To hold the breath like milk inside the body and feel the eyeballs swell and sour against bits of murky flotsam, to count in the head against re-entering the world, to exert a death wish on oneself even for twelve or fifteen seconds, to die to die below the lake and never reappear: a good dream sometimes, one that might teach infants to jettison life suddenly, imagining floating again in their parent's amniosis where breath was supplied and so, just dying. He/she would crash up to a wave of air again, gasping, wiping the bark bits from her/his eyelashes, suckling cool wind into his/her chest, smiling. Then heard the child yelp in birth, screech for dear life, and nursed it on one nipple, a sudden siphon, a parent-beast smelling of sweat and blood and triumph, and the child's tiny fingers and puckered earlobes still shedding gummy white vernix and tight determined gums pumping and prying.

3   Constantinople was a thick-wristed dyke/fag who liked to banana-ride a rickety skateboard to his/her dayjob at the contemporary photography gallery and then pitch dirt from the square plot she/he'd drawn on a patch of dry swamp to clear a basement for his/her future cabin around which she/he'd rein a half-dozen nags saved from the glue factory and whistle Pavarotti/Mouskouri into the spectral glimmer of a frost-tinged October evening. She/he drank tequila. He/she dreamt hard fucks yet crumpled under a firm hand set to penetrate her/his own scared and unhumid

asshole. He/she sidled up in thick jeans. She/he baked like a vegan fiend, smoked pot and fried hemp and liked to wake up with a really good hangover. He/she left redneck siblings to their own subdivisions and wrote her/his Alzheimer's-stolen mother/father once a month on flowered stationery in a curvaceous delicate script and sometimes enclosed a pressed violet for the scent and the delicate physical presence it embued as it flittered onto the confused geezer/old lady's bedspread. She/he paid for his/her own housecleaner. He/she pumped weights at the Y. Her/his navel was pierced with a copper helix but no one could so much as breathe on his/her tits or she/he'd yank the offender by the collar onto a leatherette barstool and over-the-shoulder frisbee it into ferocious upbrading rotation. Simmer down, he/she'd snarl, know your boundaries or else be prepared to suffer some pretty unique consequences with me, a kind of pickup line that flopped with some but worked like a charm with the rabidly needy ones who awaited a chance to be boxed off into a time-out for any minor infraction of the flesh.

4   She/he could not sleep and instead sat up batting mosquitos and masturbating. The soft wetted penis/clitoris grew with her/his hand's concentric encouragement to the hallucinatory rootlessness of an adult navel or the yummy bulb of an erect clit/cock or the licked lump of an eyelid. A vacuous eternity of night swirled around in his/her mind agitating the immeasurably friendly and benign drift of autumnal sky perforated by the sparkle of stars and a massive orange three-quarter moon that cast a blue-silvered stripe across the lake's rippling scale. This was landscape's itinerant desire spotlit for all those who pretend its irrelevance in the globalist fury for cash and status and virtual profit. She/he was full of hope outside that screen as his/her cunt/cock began to swell and pulse and the canal inside/outside her/him began its emergent shape-shift toward a certain density of presence shared by the body's other vital organs, an embedded auto-erectile insistence of the interior self straining in a circulating preordainment through skin to the vast thirst of air outside

him/her, as though the entire room were sucking her/him off, drawing in the fat slick projectility of tissue to a suspended peak of hunger for its own explosion, its own expulsion of gelatinous ejaculate onto the apricot-coloured sheet and sweat-dampened sleeve of the room's air. Breathing quiet then, drowsing, for the morning would appear as it always did and the neighbour's sad dog would lope off-kilter to the camp's doorstoop demanding a scattering of milk biscuits and a winsome pat or two on his/her mongrel-red shoulder.

So what were Y O U doing, she/he would demand of the lanky rust-banged mail deliverer when he/she emerged from around the terrace side of the cottage, nowhere near the mailbox, and removed her/his navy blue cap and grinned, It's me, the doggie you like to pet, treat to cookies, in virile human form! And he/she stammered, Why you, why you are joking with my humour and don't you know I only like you for the pretty envelopes you carry into my purview? The pathetic bubble-poof of unmasked magic snapped her/him back into canine miserableness and his/her overheated teat/shlong hung down like a dopey vagrant tail her/his owner had forgotten to trim and/or delouse, leaving him/her alone again in a self-aroused routine of normal tasks. She/he liked the hum of the fridge and could always coax the local wheel of the radio for company and brew coffee and stare outside at the radiant day's spattering, splintering light.

5   The oval-shaped garden of rose bushes had gone to messy hell with half-dead and/or semi-alive brown-rimmed petals drooping or falling or having landed and been shmushed by one of the groundskeepers' reinforced boot toes. Those lazy sons/daughters of bitches/bastards collected their pensions and spat gobs of regurgitated mucus in polka-dottish pattern on the sedimentary rockface as if there were not even an odd job to be found among the fledgling weeds and wild grasses. They stomped unawares. Why were they not fucking fired a long while ago? He/she would do it, would flatter them with walking papers, for a garden should be coddled

116

and parsed, inspected with the fingertips and sniffed appreciatively, just as a baby's rough patches required lotion and tut-tutting and the pathetic celibate's genitalia deserved an expert finicky tickle, did they not? Sometimes it is politically key to oust the incumbent, for his/her ideas have become separated out, a cupful of butter abandoned to the heat, all the creamy cholesterol-packed desirables solidifying to a lowest-common-denominator Canadian Shield atop the translucent always liquid whey which in this case can be taken to portray life's essential lubrificants, tonics to enliven people to their own porous sentience but to the lip of which they are too greasy to get. Does she/he have an inkling of how to hire help that makes a difference? He/she can't stand to garden and all the living, lurching shoots about her/him applaud as the wind sings through their clever green jackets for they are dressed nicely for the pre–Strawberry Social recital and the blue curtain of afternoon's hymen/foreskin has just (sshh, really? now!) been gashed.

6   A seventeen-year-old daughter/son somewhere else in the world (?) while he/she sat hard on her/his soft ass staring at the economical lake water convey itself to sand then swallow its thrust and gently spool off to the blue distance it came from, a loop arriving and rushing away (bad guest) without accepting so much as a glass of apple juice or palmful of Ripple Lays to ritualize its meaning here on the human shore. A renegade fringe of lake casts itself against the exotic beach in momentary indignation but always prefers and defends return to its homogeneous liquid home, so apart from the detachment- and discretion-based society of the oxygen suckers. He/she is stuck on objects, one by one, on how different each seems, on how very special and unique the small collapsible bones of a curled fist are when recalled from a distance of a dozen and a half years, on this or that palpable mammary/teste, on the plate of just-cooked food that balances protein, carbohydrate and fibre in tertiary colour composition, on the purple loosestrife so elegant and calm by the burbling creek, on the dropped beach towel that mimics an erratic S on the parched

grass, on the soccer ball by the small cedar, on the purple and white beachball hidden in the shadow of the old rickety swingset, on the yellow-and-blue-star-patterned stuffed cloth ball rounding from a dug sandbank, on the bench, the toe, the pen, the book, the helicopter up there, there above the mating bluebottles, sapphire glints, and the big white boathouse plopped directly across the lake with something, a stain or a scrape modulating its longest lovely white flank. She/he can jump in the lake for all he/she cares for the past; it harms her/him to think on it too long, challenges a godlike eminence to speak up about how beautiful and how brutal is the lake's lateral narrative where nothing is left or lost but all is absorbed into its shimmering only-too-pleased-seeming skin.

7   Harvest today: a cupful or raspberries and one green bean. Tomatoes will wait two or three more days and one can only pluck as many zucchinis as it is probable to imagine consuming without wincing remorse. Why break the stem sooner than essential? The extravagant golden blossoms of the parent plants are fancy-bouquet – no, deluxe-banquet – ready. But each petal will crumple and retract and curl until it resembles an ancient cigarette as yellow as the skinny fingers that roll their own and smoke incessantly, and then these left-behind papery tubes will moult and turn to compost crushed with the raggedy dregs of broad once-green zucchini leaves, in the garden patch, while eight or ten or twenty of the vegetable will be chopped and fried and sliced and breaded and cut raw for crudité trays that feature homegrown garden favourites …

He/she is able to write.

8   When the overhead bulblight brightens her/his little seat, the plugged-in teenaged boy/girl in the seat across settles both trigger-pointed hands from their deejay-turntable-scratch mania and begins to resist the kinetic incantatory semaphore of the back of her/his gelled skull beating a deaf

mimicry of Missy Elliott/Eminem against the bus's paisley headrest. But given a segue of two or three minutes, he/she resumes his ear-fed program of physiocultish gestures, poking and slicing the air in front of her/his small intestine, mouthing cartoonish curt warnings and abrupt air dots and dashes with the panache of a MuchMusic champ. He/she does it all without leaking a groan or hiss or hum or ba-ba-bah, controlling better than a stocktrader the adolescent reflex to contract and expand and contract-expand. At least her/his disciplined body moves itself in the night on the bus in the cover of motional dark or, even, in the light.

9   And then there is the return and the return again, back to the city which loses everything at 4:11 one radiant yellow afternoon, and so back to the lake where energy replenishes its own grass-scented appetite and loons duck and ducks loop and a young catfish is absconded to a bucket from a swamp and the children perk up at its funny feline whiskers as it skitters in cloudy frantic purgatory, giddy as a kitten except for an implicit panic shared by all creatures grabbed (even kindly) from their origins and set to circle in a plastic pail. Oxygen is not enough for a decent life, no, one can gather the desire for return and refine its slick blue-oiled feathers and fashion a cable through which the readied shafts, lined up one after the next, shoot, sailing each on its flight path home like a single heroic spasmotic sperm or stretchy ovulatory jelly discharge caught by the wadded fleece of a gym sock held tight to snuff fourteen-year-old lust from the presence of an eavesdropping babysitter. Why is it hard to bear the individual's trueheart greed, his or her propellant need which scripts all hope into a score of actions that displace some other dream from its marshside amble? If you wish to fuck yourself, fine, yet soon swims the premise of another organism, ballooning its own plump cheeks to find the stuff it wants to feed on, to be filled by, or to fuck in cascading jolts of forward-moving impulse, and where will the excess power-rush crash if that one pure wish is stunted or shut out? A catastophe is what evolves of a catfish, O poor little catfish!, when scooped up for a take-home trophy

of certain poster kids' nature hunts, who search apostle-like for their own essence in among the cattails and sunfish. O, error! O, horny toads galumphing by the cottage's back patio, hiding in the shadow of the gas-powered barbecue, charading the wallflower wattage of stones.

10   During this retreat she/he began to love sex again, to think of it often, to suggest it at random and call it up from driftwood shapes in the late afternoon woods where sun jiggles through maple and poplar arbours so that lozenges of brightness and darkness giddily toggle each other's hit-switches, upending and perforating the idea of edges, of whose belong where, of which skin should fix isolates or lodge units in apt historical order. He/she mouthfucked and assfucked and swam in the nude, suckled on blueberries and swallowed traffic jams, counted dippers and asterisked skin flicks for future viewing. The slow-jerking queue of red taillights back to the metropolis glistened its meadow of shiny ripe plucks. She/he licked his/her cheeks and stroked shins, so tanned and soft and continuous that night as the bus stammered its way back while the languid dark highway moaned, Fuck me now, just fuck me.

11   Travelling at a near standstill by the Georgian Downs, just south of Barrie, one considers that there are curious lacunae in the English language. For example, what possible explanation can be given for the non-existence of the seemingly sound word *slets*. Think of it, all its sister/fellow words have a vibrant upmarket portfolio: slats, slits, slots and sluts. Why stall on slets? Lest we laze by a shuttered window and blink at the silver mini-Niagara of our good luck when, in a striped halter and backless stilettos, Pamela Anderson (all ooman) appears on a primetime segment of a Hep C television benefit to remind us how the bloodworn disease always sneaks through a slack pore of rotten lust or poor hygiene, we must believe it and believe in it, or else let us tell some better statistics about profiting from loss at the lit-up casino: Be stealthy, have some slets about you, when

teasing fate. And still though the falls gush, expect not free money to coin its own phase in your future – i.e., raise blinders not blinds and always use a sharp letter opener when corresponding with the lost loves of your youth!

12   There are certain days when she/he desires to write about the body. On others: his/her body. To which do the asshole, the tits, the balls, the cunt belong? Forcing a shuttlecock from side to side, quick, between two racquets raised for the arrival of sensation and sense: What springs to life at the mention of touch, how the word arcs and bobs in the air on its path to making contact with skin, brain, palette of the outthrust tongue, bounces to the back of the throat and is gulped like sex into the sanctum of her/himself, the low tucked-inside moist pad secreting juices and scent and muscling urges. Is she or he inside or outside identity when he or she stuffs it in her or him, crossing hairs and siting a soon-felt separateness wherein and so far as he/she can tell, the simmering body misses its limits? Stir the body already, stir him/her into it.

To make a gesture of retreat and re-entry. Unlike the wind or rock or sand clogged with water at the edge of the lake, or even weather's constant shifts which remove static from the picture. To masturbate is to set the body his/her swirls in motion clockwise and lengthwise and with the hand's fingers to rub and strum the kettle's metal side bright with buoyancy and how the midst of her/him rises to the shape of whatever he/she's thinking.

WAITING

Breasts still make out
the presence of the distant

The main feature of a good short story is that
it winds out or will wend not too far off

in the future from when it began to be read
or heard Doesn't matter how long while taken for the

author to write; what matters is quantity time standard
reader will need to donate The ideal short story departs

enthuses and finalizes in under one third of an hour
Can be had happily on lunch breaks along with nutritious

lunch and a walk If some walk is shut out
this should be due to (inclement) weather or a meeting

directly after lunch at which it would sit incorrect to
have patches of sweat under the arms If lunch itself

is not possible to eat alongside the story for example
if the story harbours a surfeit of images of vomiting

or of monstrous snaps of violence or deprivation such that
the reader cannot also inundate while reading this is not

a remarkable story though it may couch within the time
criteria If the story shocks or carouses some reader to

such vesicular inflated vagary that the story's effects will not
be packed away promptly neither is it a good short

story for a good one goes into the reader and
holds her there working its turns inside her until she's

roundly roundly dispensed to its virtuals and then a good
one gets up and goes so she can regroup to

work where she is recompensed and required to be She
does not own all day after all Now the thing

about Viagra is that some men have attached themselves very
hard to the idea that all sundial and all nightshade

would be the best curiosity of time to develop one
short story into an elongated text no one will soon

obviate I say however sorry If I can't masticate lunch
what is the point of the winding stroll to the

planetarium and fro and who will be reminding the crème
caramel Prehensile children must be picked up and uncoiled to

the dental hygienist School correctives must be signed if double-signed
Picture windows must be disinfected with balsamics On the day

my first offspring was born – just before dinnertime it was
and she radial daughter – I caught view of a clock

Thirty-three hours had turned inside me each as though clicking
the spoke of a carnival-game wheel since the spill of

amniotic waters all over the carpet Uncommon completeness of day
plus a third again and she the girl was spirally

arrived Outdrawn story of the world Sweet good garlanded with
bloodied cord garnet sewage placenta the mass of Steak for

Two very very rare That is time attending Its memory
careens in the cunt even now Windows inaugurate A train

clangs by pulling sixty-three containers half red and brown the
others a motley assortment of dingy and rusted-out bargain pink

Close up swell elegant birch trunk phallic and patient the
ideal totem Curled knots like ashen vaginas a woodpecker comes

to pound and suckle Behind fan after fan of supple
green flickering leaves a thousand mouths cheerfully egging on cool

updraft So damn enthusiastic said foliage Time seems but a
blizzard in one of those shake 'em up souvenirs with the cabin

scene and a bear on his back legs roaring You
thought I'd forgotten you You didn't percolate the faith You

need to stew some trove some breed some Here I
squat with my knickers down about my clavicle crushing the

bathroom break Lunch a walk the story and a freshen-up
in the grotty stall are all required by the quality

forty minutes allowed to union employees I haven't decided yet
when I'll terminate but I'll dedicate and get severance you'll

discover The line that divides the future from the just-past
is per course endemic to the stall door operable by

its curious round stainless-steel lock and one firm quarter-turn
upward That door swings in fast clips you on the

nostril your whole long spine jerks like a snapped branch
in the forest – you compose zipper wiping wayward urine upper

each hind pocket of your jeans (it's Casual Friday) and
stride out Fresh Fresh fresh fresh One look in the

vast fingerprinted mirror and you verify no one will ever
frick you again You're exquisite ruin Your exeunt poster self

shimmers in the silvery flotation device you keep forever as
hepcat flotsam on middle brain whose unoxidized cells are accumulating

in a flake pyramid like runaway deposit of mealy ant
dung Who would wish to idle twenty minutes with exhibited

naked torso? Who would anteriorize mallow thighs and gleefully enter?
Now prime thing about woodpeckers is they cherish their privacy

Species hate the chug of the train rounding the pass
They sacred-make how their great-great-great-grandmother was crushed no
splattered against

the tooting blue caboose of a lumber-loaded convoy bound for
the southwest markets Souls recall the purpled-blood explosion of her

venerable chest smeared inside-out on the conductor's windshield and such
astonished beakless face sucking in fear like gooseberries currants milkweed

mixed in cyclone Bertha Then out it comes on his
swipe of the glass rather heaved confection pocked with uneven

lumps of early-morning toast and bangers Instantaneous conjugate of the
red no-longer-bird plus taupe deliver-us-from-human for thine butters the blasted

windowpane Through rude spew I can still see the clock
plodding determinedly past the halfway point My pace palpitates My

wish to stop in at the A&P and sneak a
suck of a pack of smokes is stifled Wind tinkles

chimes and east sky has brightened One puffy triangular cumulus
struts an Adonis kilter hips torqued knees and elbows jauntily

bent square bricks of chest side-staring brow Wild craven sky
full of people making sex and laughing Us poor pink-collars

gnarled at space-age desks having e-mail and suppressing gas Then
there's Charlie whose so-rock-stiff-it's-blue erection is holding work
exceedingly tough

He knows Viagra is against regulations for union employees He
initialled also submitted the contractual one-sheet circulated en masse in

an unlabelled beige folder with its urgent adjunct clause 18.3
re Erectile Enhancers and the Safe Envelope Keeping Our Workplace

at Half-Mast Thus Happy but he could not carry through
on the collective repression His is throbbing in this seat

with three hours to go before afternoon coffee break Time
is on verily cunt The clock apparitions to move counter

to nature into the past into his torso pressing turns
in his body that elongate and linger It is not

good though and neither is it short I am not
bothered by any pornographic obsessions of my workmates Genders are

only human They spurt unsurprisingly animal When ripe carmine placenta
arrives you persevere you have delivered a tender organ one

you did not know you could enable and live to
cistern the story You cozy to weep and then fit

the infant onto your breast hard as a winter apple
nipple terse as a screw as nubile as marathon length

of your life to this fresh harsh threshed beginning You
are lunch Will sit supped You are transparent turquoise hourglass

fragile measure-sifter Blue train rounding an illegible pass whistling loudly
to warn the woodpeckers No longer advertise where any girl

has her end and you your stall door swinging inward
Time tall in you like every erectile birch still untickled

but all green leaves flutter quill quaver and make a
semaphore of a thousand short right stories to render each

forested enough to stay every through to the proximate knothole
where all can suckle and pound for self again Short

is not this contract Good is not exact probe Should
is more point it Gorging on you is the kid

Exercise book flops in your lap and who knows how
you can hold the pen when she heaves off and

kickles you On his strict lunch break your flagrant husband
guesses it is time for a quickie Yellow bird flaps

and rattles at the windshield Searing clouds perk up their
quadrilateral chest blocks Distance thunders some bad weather on satellite

Sun patches sweat under your armpits; I am humid I
wait for you to finish so shortly I can curl

up with you The main feature is I want to
curl up with you I want to be curling up

with you Did you my window think I had forgotten
Now I rasp gentle Now simple day air softened heat's

blunt fingers Now I regarded my girlie skinny-dipping in old
fuss lake Now I moaned like a night train reaming

out a poplar grove Now I smelled fish and mentally
removed a dead shrew from the shore Now I hated

my mother who would not come near me Now I
coffee-fondanted one third of a cake Now sand stigmatized into

cracks of everything Now it admitted all merely so la-di-da
Honestly who intends to wade deeper when the lake circles

its hips like that despite all verdant evidence of violence
chugging at the pass suckling knotholes except waiting waiting Waiting

NOTES AND ACKNOWLEDGEMENTS

'Lucent' appeared in *The Capilano Review* in Winter 2005. Thanks to editor Sharon Thesen. With fondness for SM.

'Lection' appeared in *Rampike* in 2005.

'Photo' was published in *NO: A Journal of the Arts*.

'Lease' appeared in the December/January 2004/05 issue of *The Walrus*.

An earlier version of 'Cure' was published in *The Fiddlehead*.

'An Honest Offer' was published in *The Common Sky: Canadian Writers Against the War* (Three Squares Press).

'The Problem' appears on the Foreign Correspondents page (edited by Meredith Quartermain and Jacqueline Turner) of Meredith Quartermain's website <www.interchg.ubc.ca/quarterm>. As well, a version was published in a chapbook produced by Gustave Morin for the Windsor Festival of the Book 2004 as a takeaway for the 'Quote Experimental Unquote' evening.

'Grief' appears within a longer sequence in *White Wall Review*, Summer 2005. Tendered for MJM.

Thanks to Don McKay for reflections on the wild of poetry, which contributed to my thinking for 'Explaining Landscape Painting to the Activist.'

'School' was published in *Prism* in July 2004. This poem is a subjective translation of a generated French text culled from an art historical monograph on the sixteenthth-century painters of l'Ecole de Fontainbleau. Equalities, sonorities and liberties have been tasted throughout. For DDC.

'Uncertain Instincts,' 'Connotations (Overland Version),' 'The Groin Area (Wet Version)' and 'Filterless (Soft Version)' appeared in *Small Press Traffic Review*, San Francisco, in Fall 2005. Thanks to Bryan Gee for introducing me to Anthony Minghella's short film, via the Internet.

'An Open Erotics of Gzowski' was published in *cv2*. Contrary perhaps to majority opinion, the author found Peter Gzowski's voice sexy and misses it still.

Written in Sudbury in August 2003, 'Retreat Diary' was published in *The Windsor Review*, Spring 2004, and as a limited-edition chapbook by Book Thug in late 2004. 'Waiting,' written a year later on the same lake property, was also included in the BookThug chapbook. Many thanks to Jay MillAr.

This work was written from early 2002 through Spring 2005.

Funding through the Ontario Arts Council, the Toronto Arts Council and the Canada Council Writing Residency program in collaboration with the University of Windsor, as well as extended family resources, allowed me the time and space to write.

Thanks to the exiled writers I met and learned from – and to Maggie Helwig and Elizabeth Ruth for their support – during my time as Readers and Writers coordinator at PEN Canada, March 2003 to April 2004.

Thank you to Freda Martin, Zoë Henderson and my sister, Demetra Christakos, and dear friends Victoria Freeman and Mark Fawcett, for being here.

Many thanks to my colleagues in the University of Windsor English Department over 2004–2005, in particular Di Brandt, Susan Holbrook and Darryl Whetter. Gratitude to excellent students in the Creative Writing program for testing my chops.

Thanks to Diana Fitzgerald Bryden, Ann Shin, Saghi Ghahraman, Cynthia Leroy, Mark Cochrane, Rachel Zolf and Darren Wershler-Henry for helpful responses to my work at various points during its writing and editing. Thanks also to Bill Kennedy, Angela Rawlings and many other remarkable bright movers in the Toronto writing community for perpetuating innovative poetry as public culture.

Many thanks and much respect to my editor for the press, Kevin Connolly, and Coach House editor Alana Wilcox. Thanks to Darren Wershler-Henry for the text design. Also to Jason McBride, Christina Palassio, Stan Bevington and everyone else at the Coach House, thanks for your terrific work.

Abiding thanks to the wonderful bpNichol, a still most-present mentor, and to my forever-phantoms William Steig, Gertrude Stein, Louise Bourgeois and David Murray.

Ongoing gratitude and love to Bryan Gee – with thanks also for the gorgeous cover design – and to our terrific, bright-spirited, patient kids Zephyr, Silas and Clea Christakos-Gee.

Typeset in Laurentian and Gill Sans
Printed and bound at the Coach House on bpNichol Lane, 2005

Edited for the press by Kevin Connolly
Cover by Bryan Gee, in collaboration with the author
Photo of the author by Bryan Gee

Coach House Books
401 Huron Street rear on bpNichol Lane
Toronto, Ontario
M5S 2G5
416 979 2217 • 1 800 367 6360
mail@chbooks.com
www.chbooks.co